AFRICAN AMERICAN SUPERSTARS

LIZZO

C.R. MCKAY

New York

Published in 2022 by The Rosen Publishing Group, Inc.
29 East 21st Street, New York, NY 10010

Copyright © 2022 by The Rosen Publishing Group, Inc.

All rights reserved. No part of this book may be reproduced in any form without permission in writing from the publisher, except by a reviewer.

First Edition

Editor: Greg Roza
Designer: Rachel Rising

Photo Credits: Cover, p. 1 Frazer Harrison/Staff/Getty Images Entertainment/Getty Images; pp. 4, 6, 8, 10, 12, 14, 16, 18, 20, 21 Woskresenskiy/shutterstock.com; pp. 4, 6, 8, 10, 12, 14, 16, 18, 20, 21 Sunward Art/shutterstock.com; p. 5 Axelle/Bauer-Griffin/Contributor/FilmMagic/Getty Images; p. 7 Theo Wargo/Staff/Getty Images Entertainment/Getty Images; p. 9 Matt Jelonek/Contributor/WireImage/Getty Images; p. 10 Boris Medvedev/Shutterstock.com; p. 11 JEAN-BAPTISTE LACROIX/Contributor/AFP/Getty Images; p. 13 Star Tribune via Getty Images/Contributor/Star Tribune/Getty Images; p. 15 Sam Santos/Contributor/WireImage/Getty Images; p. 17 Don Arnold/Stringer/Getty Images Entertainment/Getty Images; p. 19 Alberto E. Rodriguez/Stringer/Getty Images Entertainment/Getty Images; p. 21 Steve Granitz/Contributor/WireImage/Getty Images.

Library of Congress Cataloging-in-Publication Data

Names: McKay, C. R. (writer of juvenile literature) author.
Title: Lizzo / C. R. McKay.
Description: New York : PowerKids Press, 2022. | Series: African American superstars | Includes index.
Identifiers: LCCN 2020036533 | ISBN 9781725326118 (hardcover) | ISBN 9781725326095 (paperback) | ISBN 9781725326101 (6 pack)
Subjects: LCSH: Lizzo, 1988–Juvenile literature. | Singers–United States–Biography–Juvenile literature. | Rap musicians–United States–Biography–Juvenile literature.
Classification: LCC ML3930.L579 M35 2022 | DDC 782.42164092 [B]–dc23
LC record available at https://lccn.loc.gov/2020036533

Manufactured in the United States of America

CPSIA Compliance Information: Batch #CSPK22. For Further Information contact Rosen Publishing, New York, New York at 1-800-237-9932.

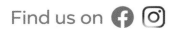

CONTENTS

Lizzo in the Spotlight 4

Growing Up 6

Becoming Lizzo 8

Lizzo in College 10

Hard Times 12

Flying Solo 14

World Famous 16

Winning Big and
Giving Back 18

Lizzo the Superstar 20

Glossary 22

For More Information 23

Index 24

Lizzo in the Spotlight

Lizzo is a singer. She writes songs and raps. She also plays the flute. She has big shows all over the world. She tells her fans they should love themselves—just the way they are.

Growing Up

Lizzo's real name is Melissa Viviane Jefferson. She was born in Detroit, Michigan, on April 27, 1988. She has two older **siblings**. Her family moved to Houston, Texas, when she was 10 years old.

Becoming Lizzo

Lizzo started playing the flute when she was in sixth grade. She and two of her classmates formed a rap group. She got the name Lizzo from the nickname Lissa and the Jay-Z song "Izzo."

Lizzo in College

Lizzo went to the University of Houston. She studied music. She also played **piccolo** in the Cougar marching band. The flute is still important to Lizzo. She plays flute during her shows. She named her flute Sasha Flute.

piccolo

11

Hard Times

Lizzo dropped out of college by her junior year. She slept on friends' floors and couches. She also lived out of her car for six months. Her parents had moved to Denver, Colorado. Then, her father died in 2009.

Flying Solo

In 2011, Lizzo moved to Minneapolis, Minnesota. She was in a few bands. One of the bands worked on a song with the music **legend** Prince. She also worked on **solo** projects. In 2013, she put out her first album.

World Famous

Lizzo's music is one of a kind. It's a mix of pop, rap, and **R&B**. She writes her own songs. Her songs are about her life. Her song "Truth Hurts" hit it big. This song made her world famous.

Winning Big and Giving Back

In 2019 and 2020, Lizzo's songs climbed to the top of the music charts. She won three Grammy Awards. She gave back too. Lizzo helped people hurt by wildfires in Australia. She also spoke out about **climate change**.

Lizzo the Superstar

Lizzo's new sound and bold songs are changing rap and **hip-hop**. She teaches self-love no matter your size or color. Lizzo is a superstar with a big voice—and a bright future.

TIMELINE

April 27, 1988	Lizzo is born.
October 15, 2013	Lizzo puts out her first album.
2014	Lizzo works with music legend Prince.
2017	Lizzo puts out her hit song "Truth Hurts."
2019	Lizzo puts out her hit album *Cuz I Love You*.
2020	Lizzo wins three Grammy Awards.

GLOSSARY

climate change: Change in Earth's weather caused by human activity.

hip-hop: Music relating to rap and similar styles.

legend: Someone who is famous for a special trait, such as musical skill.

piccolo: A musical instrument that looks like a small flute and plays very high notes.

R&B: Rhythm and blues. A type of music that arose from African American music of the 1940s and led to the rise of rock and roll.

sibling: A brother or sister.

solo: Of or relating to making music on one's own.

FOR MORE INFORMATION

BOOKS

Latchana Kenney, Karen. *Lizzo: Award-Winning Musician.* Mankato, MN: Capstone, 2021.

Wilson, Lakita. *Lizzo: Breakout Artist.* Minneapolis, MN: Lerner Publications, 2020.

WEBSITES

Britannica Kids: Hip-Hop

kids.britannica.com/kids/article/hip-hop/399968

Learn more about hip-hop, including its history and legends.

Kidzworld: Lizzo Fun Facts

www.kidzworld.com/article/31589-lizzo-fun-facts

Visit this website to learn much more about Lizzo.

Publisher's note to parents and teachers: Our editors have reviewed the websites listed here to make sure they're suitable for students. However, websites may change frequently. Please note that students should always be supervised when they access the internet.

INDEX

A
album, 14, 22

D
Detroit, Michigan, 6

F
family, 6, 12
flute, 4, 8, 10

G
Grammy Awards, 18, 22

H
Houston, Texas, 6

M
Minneapolis, Minnesota, 14

P
piccolo, 10
Prince, 14, 22

R
rap, 4, 8, 16, 20
R&B, 16

T
"Truth Hurts," 16, 22